The Closer's 21 Proven Secrets To Close More Wholesale Deals In 30 Days With No Sales Experience

TONY "THE CLOSER" ROBINSON

ISBN: 9781731015150

DEDICATION

This book is dedicated to my parents,
Anthony Sr. and Beverly Robinson.

You taught so much and the life I have today
is because of what I learned from you.

Thank you.

CONTENTS

NOT ANOTHER BOOK
ABOUT WHOLESALING!?!

Do you love to do wholesale deals and want to do more? Or maybe you've done a couple of deals (or tried to do them) but struggled?

Maybe you thought you knew how to wholesale but then you get in front of a motivated seller and suddenly you don't know what to say… or the seller throws you a curveball… or think you've done everything necessary but the seller won't agree to the deal.

What then?

You'll be relieved to know that you're not alone. This happens to many investors, every single day! And many investors are left wondering what they did wrong and what information they're missing from the wholesaling process.

Well, here's the part that most investors mix up:

You probably don't need to know anything else about wholesaling. If you got in front of the seller and had all the forms ready, then you were probably fully equipped to do the deal from a technical perspective… you're not missing any other wholesaling details.

That's why I didn't write a book about wholesaling. There are a lot of books and experts out there who can give you the step-by-step details about how to do wholesale deals.

But if you've ever wondered why there are so many wholesaling experts but still so many wholesalers struggle to do deals, I'll let you in on a little secret: it's not the wholesaling information that's lacking… it's the wholesaler's knowledge, skills, and confidence in closing the deal.

You know how to WHOLESALE… the invisible struggle that many wholesalers face is how to CLOSE!

That's what I teach, and that's what this book is all about: it's about helping you get to the next level in your wholesaling… not by giving you more technical detail but by showing you how to close the deal once you're face-to-face with a seller. You'll be surprised at how simple and straightforward it can be to do more deals.

HOW I DISCOVERED
THE POWER OF CLOSING

My name is Tony Robinson. People call me "The Closer"... but I wasn't always a closer. In fact, I never really dreamed of being an investor at all!

My parents, Anthony Sr. and Beverly Robinson, were amazing people who taught me the value of hard work. They inspired me and encouraged me to work hard and always go toward my dreams. I studied Business Administration at Carson Newman College and graduated from there in 2005 and went on to play professional football. In 2006, I was an undrafted free agent with the Seattle Seahawks.

After my football career, I was looking for my next opportunity, so I turned to the automotive industry and chose a career in the sales department of Hendrick Automotive Group, the largest privately owned group of car dealerships in the US (owned by the Rick Hendrick, who also owns several trophy-winning NASCAR teams).

The dealership took a chance on me even though I was an untested sales rookie. Even though I'd never sold a car in my life, I sold over 23 my first month at the dealership. I went on to be the Top Salesperson in the Hendrick Automotive Group from 2008 to 2011 and was inducted into exclusive clubs for top salespeople, including the Chairman's Club and the President's Club.

After a successful career in automotive sales, I went on to coach the top real estate investors in the country, which is something I still do (and love to do!) today. Over the years I closed more than 1000 deals and generated over $10 million in sales.

I'm not telling you any of this to impress you. Rather, I'm telling you this so you realize something: some people might look at what I achieved (or how quickly I achieved it) even without any background or experience in sales, and they might assume that it was LUCK.

It was not luck at all. It was skill: skills honed on-the-fly at the Hendrick Automotive Group... skills I even used in football... skills I didn't learn in college as well as skills I "hacked" from my Masters in Psychology... skills I learned from my hardworking parents that I could apply when working with people, whether I was face-to-face with a prospective car buyer or with a motivated seller.

In this book, I'll share my best-proven closing strategies with you and show you how to use them to close more wholesale deals.

Ready? Let's get started...

CLOSING SECRET #1
CHANGE YOUR MINDSET

Many investors get into wholesaling because they love the opportunity it provides to achieve financial freedom. Then they learn the technical information about how to wholesale and they think they're ready… but then when they are face-to-face with a motivated seller, they discover an aspect of wholesaling that they didn't realize: to be successful in wholesaling, you need to become great at selling. (After all, you're selling to a motivated seller the reasons that they should do a deal with you!)

… And this is where a lot of wholesalers get stuck because people don't like the idea of selling.

Let me ask you: what do you think of when I mention the word "selling"? Most people think "ewww" and they get a look on their face as if they just drank expired milk. For many people, selling seems pushy or even unethical. Maybe you think of those stereotypical used car salesmen in bad suits who try to push you into a car and then sell you the over-priced rust protection, or maybe you think of the telemarketers who just won't get off the phone. Unfortunately, a few pushy or unethical salespeople have given a bad name to the millions of helpful and ethical salespeople. (That's the reason I tend to avoid using the word "sales" at all and instead talk about "closing"—even though that's a sales term, it doesn't have the same negative connotations.)

Here's what you must realize: when a salesperson is selling to you in an ethical, non-pushy way, you don't even realize he or she is selling to you. You may not even realize you are talking to a salesperson!

Why? Because selling the right way is helping. Yes! Selling is helping:

- It's helping the other person dig deeper into their own situation
- It's helping the other person understand their options
- It's helping the other person make a decision (since many people struggle with decision-making)
- It's helping the other person solve a huge problem in their life

Selling the right way is ethical and not pushy; rather, it's helping the other person achieve their goals. Think about a time that you helped a friend who needed to make a decision. You helped them think through the pros and cons of their choices, you shared your opinion with them, and then they made a decision. You sold them (even though you didn't realize you were selling) because you were helping them.

And that is exactly why I love wholesaling! Motivated sellers are struggling with a huge, confusing (and expensive) problem with their house and they need experts like you and I to help them.

As a wholesaler, you can be a great seller to motivated sellers by helping them solve the big complicated problem they're facing with their house. It all starts with adjusting your mindset.

First, be aware that great wholesaling is actually selling.

Second, change what you think about selling and realize that it is actually helping.

Everything else in this book is built on this first secret of changing what you think about selling. If you don't change your mindset, everything else will be a struggle and you will not do as many deals as you'd like to do. But if you realize that wholesaling is selling, and that selling is helping, you'll transform how you feel about wholesaling and how you interact with motivated sellers.

Action Steps

1. "How can I help?" is one of the most powerful phrases in the world. Make this question a key part of every conversation

you have from now on, and see what happens. The world will open up amazing opportunities for you when you ask this!

2. Start practicing today. Whenever you encounter a situation where you have to ask someone for something, start by asking, "How can I help you get what you want?"

3. Repeat to yourself every single day: "Wholesaling Is Helping." Write it on a sticky note and put that reminder where you'll see it. And, remind yourself of it before you go into a face-to-face meeting with a motivated seller.

4. Think about all the motivated sellers you have met or will meet. Consider what their problems are. Then think about what you can do or say that will help them.

Closers Take Action

Make sure you follow me on Instagram at instragram.com/trob56

Notes

_____

_____

_____

_____

_____

_____

_____

_____

_____

_____

_____

_____

CLOSING SECRET #2
UNDERSTAND WHAT CLOSING IS

I've convinced you that wholesaling is selling... and that great selling is helping. Once you change your thinking on that, you'll find a whole universe of opportunities will suddenly open up to you like never before.

Now that your mindset is correct, we can build on that foundation. The question you should be asking is: "How can I get better at selling?"

Well, Tony "The Closer" is here to help! ;) Let me make it very simple for you: a sale is made when someone makes a decision.

When I sold cars for Hendrick, other salespeople could talk and talk, and they thought they were selling, but they really weren't. The thing that made me the top salesperson from 2008 to 2011 was: I helped people make a decision... to buy a car.

In wholesaling, other wholesalers talk and talk to sellers and they think they are doing what needs to be done but they really aren't. The thing that makes me successful at wholesaling today is: I help motivated sellers make a decision... to do the wholesale deal with me.

If you want to close more wholesale deals, all four of the following must take place:

1. All of the seller's needs, wants, and problems have been understood
2. You have offered a great solution to the problems previously identified
3. You ask the seller to make a decision
4. The seller agrees

To break that down further: #1 and #2 are developed as you interact with the seller and talk to them. Many of the secrets in this book will help you achieve #1 and #2 more effectively. Then you get to #3 and this is where a lot of investors choke because they think that they shouldn't have to ask for the seller to make a decision… but you need to ask.

The reason you need to ask is: you are in control of the conversation, and the motivated seller is looking to you as the expert to help them. Without realizing it, they have allowed you to take them by the hand and walk them through the process of understanding their problems and finding a solution. Now you need to help them go all the way to the finish line by asking for them to make a decision.

The best way to ask for a decision is to simply recap everything you've covered so far, show them how your solution solves their problem, and then say one of the following phrases (you may need to cust͟   ͟slightly, depending on who you are talking to):

͟   ͟n how this can help you.

͟   ͟gh, Mr. Customer, ͟   ͟ this is for you. Will ͟   ͟"

you've said that this is ͟   ͟o, can we get started

͟   ͟d recapping what you've solution helps them, and to make a decision.

͟   ͟o this point and ask for a ͟   ͟at's okay!!! Don't be scared ͟   ͟a really valuable piece of ͟   ͟lution that the seller is happy ͟   ͟o deliver. Either way, you can ͟   ͟to learn more about their ͟   ͟em.

You are the expert. A motivated seller needs you to help them, and one of the ways you can help them is by asking them to make a decision.

Action Steps

1. Practice asking some of the closing questions above (and customize them for your situation).
2. Make a simple checklist for yourself that walks you through a typical conversation with a motivated seller. The checklist should include the information you want to know about their situation. Then, make the last point on the checklist a reminder to yourself "Present the solution and ask for a decision."

Closers Take Action

Make sure you check out my website at TonyTheCloser.com

Notes

_____

_____

_____

_____

_____

_____

_____

_____

_____

_____

CLOSING SECRET #3
GET IN THEIR FACE

As an expert wholesaler, I always advise that you use every tool available to you to do more deals. If a tool, resource, or strategy works for you, then use it to do more deals. If it doesn't work for you, then don't.

There is one tool that I think you probably should be using; unfortunately, I see a lot of wholesalers using it in the wrong way and it hurts their ability to do deals.

That tool? The phone.

Here's what I see happening: wholesalers want to do more wholesale deals and they think about how to become more efficient. They add up all that driving time and face-to-face time with a seller, and they realize that they could talk to 2-3 more sellers in the same amount of time. So these wholesalers think: "I can help 2X to 3X more sellers over the phone, and I don't need to even leave the house!"

Added to that is the fact that people hate selling or are scared of closing, so they love to hide behind the protection of a telephone instead of getting face-to-face with a seller.

The result? They don't do 2X to 3X more deals. Unfortunately, they end up doing even fewer deals. Then they scratch their heads and wonder what's wrong and they mistakenly think: "I can't do wholesale deals."

The good news is: you CAN do wholesale deals. Your struggles are not because you can't do wholesale deals... your struggles are because you're trying to use the phone when you should be face-to-face with a seller.

The phone is not a closing tool, in spite of what movies like The Wolf Of Wall Street might suggest. Sure, the phone might work for some people in some sales situations but consider this: when you talk to a seller, you are helping them in one of the most challenging situations in their life... and you are helping them deal with a house-related problem, one of the biggest purchases of their life.

Motivated sellers are desperate, scared, confused, and embarrassed. They don't want to deal with someone over the phone. When you call them, their defenses are up and they are not sure if they trust you. You can help them far more effectively when you meet them face-to-face. When you meet sellers face-to-face, you build a stronger relationship and more trust, and you show them that you care about their situation and are there to help them.

Moreover, you can't negotiate over the phone very effectively either, so when you and a seller are negotiating the price, you can't point to their roof that needs to be reshingled and work on getting a lower price.

And when a seller agrees to your deal? They can't send a contract through the phone so you have to make arrangements for them to get the contract to you... and that just adds time for them to second-guess their decision and back out of the deal.

Therefore, the phone should not be a closing tool, it should be an appointment-setting tool ONLY. Use the phone to make appointments and confirm them with the seller.

Then hang up. Then go meet the seller face-to-face. You'll build stronger relationships and instant trust. You'll be able to negotiate more effectively. And when the seller makes a decision and signs the contract, you can get that contract right away.

Result? More deals, more easily. Period. (And when that happens, you won't mind meeting face-to-face with sellers. After all, wouldn't you want to meet with the people you are trying to help?)

Action Steps

1. Create a checklist for yourself when you use the phone. Make sure the checklist only includes appointment-making talking points.

2. If sellers ask about price or other terms on the phone, bring the conversation back to how important it is to meet face-to-face so you can truly help them.

3. If you find yourself falling into the pattern of trying to close deals on the phone, write yourself a reminder note that says, "The phone is an appointment-setting tool, not a negotiation tool."

Closers Take Action

Make sure you follow me on Facebook at @TheCloser56

CLOSING SECRET #4
TALK TO DECISION-MAKERS

What would happen if you arrived home from work one day and your spouse said, "Honey, I sold the house!" or, "Honey, I just bought a car!" Would you... (1) congratulate them? (2) flip out? If you're like most people, you'd probably flip out and wonder how and why they made the decision without you! For that reason, it's quite common for salespeople to hear the words, "Let me talk to my spouse."

All you need to do is spend a day in sales and you'll discover the "secret" I'm about to share—and this is something that every person in sales learns very quickly: don't put all of your energy and effort into doing a deal until you make 100% sure that all the decision-makers are present.

Otherwise, guess what happens: you sit down with a motivated seller and you walk them through the process. You work hard to follow all the steps in this book and you're sure they're about to close... only for them to say: "Well, I need to talk to someone else who is also making the decision." That will probably lead to one of two things happening:

- Either: the other person may talk your prospect out of the deal,
- Or, you having to go back and repeat everything you said a second time.

You don't want either of those things happening! It's a huge waste of time and you'll do it once or twice and learn your lesson and never do it again. What's the better approach? Make 100% sure that every decision-maker will be present.

When you're on the phone with the motivated seller, ask them: "Who else needs to be involved in this decision? A spouse? An attorney? A relative? A co-owner?" Sometimes it could be a brother or cousin who has a financial interest in the house, or maybe it's a brother or cousin who is simply "the family's go-to advisor" for important decisions. Whatever the case may be, find out who they are and make sure they are present.

If you show up at the meeting and the decision-maker is not there, do not move forward with the meeting. Offer to reschedule. You'll save yourself a whole bunch of time and you'll prove to the sellers that you are a serious professional.

Get into the habit of asking on the phone who needs to be part of the decision-making process, and get into the habit of confirming that they will be at the meeting.

Bonus tip: If a seller says that no one else will be part of the decision, but then you get to the meeting and go through the negotiation and then the seller says they need to confer with someone else, offer to call that person together and talk to that decision-maker immediately. This is an effective way to deal with those times when sellers try to use the other decision-maker as a delaying tactic. They're usually bluffing at this point so you should call them on their bluff.

Action Steps

1. When on the phone, ask who else is needed to make a decision.
2. When confirming the appointment, or showing up at the appointment, confirm that all decision-makers will be present.

Closers Take Action

Make sure you follow me on Instagram at instragram.com/trob56

CLOSING SECRET #5
PREPARE PREPARE PREPARE

Want to know who wins 100% of all negotiations? Answer: the most prepared person. Put 2 people into a negotiation and the more prepared one will win. The reason is: the most prepared person is ready for anything and can proactively adjust their approach. The least-prepared person can only react.

When you get ready to talk to sellers, prepare. Invest time (and even some money) into preparation and you'll make more money and close more successful deals because of it.

Imagine this scenario: you get to a seller's house and you look over their house and make them an offer. Then they say, "Well I think you are not calculating that correctly because the roof doesn't need as much work as you are saying, plus houses in the area are selling for more."

Now imagine two investors who are similar situations. One investor says: "umm, yes, well, uhhh… let me go back to my office and crunch some numbers and let's set up another meeting." While another investor says: "Your roof doesn't seem to need a lot of work but I have quotes from roofing companies for your size of roof and I'm using the average price for these quotes, plus the houses in the neighborhood that are selling for more are houses that have newer furnaces than you have. Plus the economy has declined by 10% since most of the other houses in the neighborhood have sold, so we can expect a lower selling price anyway."

It's a no-brainer: the second investor will get that deal because they were prepared! What a difference preparation makes!

So, what should you prepare? Everything!

- Prepare your own negotiation skills by reading and re-reading this book and practicing your negotiation skills.
- Prepare your knowledge of the area by looking at what other houses in the area are selling for. (Talk to an agent to get comps, if necessary.)
- Prepare a list of costs that people have to pay when selling through an agent versus selling to you directly.
- Prepare by looking into your sellers—by making assumptions about who they are by what they do and their family or work situation, but also by looking at their social media accounts. Find the emotional hot buttons that may make them more convinced to do a deal with you.
- Prepare your ability to negotiate by practicing with others to hone your skills.
- Prepare a list of dozens of questions to ask a seller to get to know them.
- Prepare a list of prices for typical repairs needed around the house.
- Prepare a list of current neighborhood prices and how long those houses have been on the market.
- Prepare a list of objections that a seller might have when talking to you, and prepare your answers to those objections to help them see that you can help them.
- Prepare with some forecasts of what the economy will be like in the future, plus other important factors that may convince them to act now instead of waiting.

Action Steps

1. Using the list above, prepare the information so it's at your fingertips during your next meeting with a seller.
2. After every negotiation (whether you closed or not) ask yourself: "How could I have prepared differently to end up with a better outcome?"

Closers Take Action

Make sure you check out my website at TonyTheCloser.com

CLOSING SECRET #6
RESEARCH THE SELLER

Technically you did some of this work in the previous Closing Secret but it's so important that I wanted to call it out as a key secret all on its own. This one will make or break the success of your negotiation!

Research the seller before you meet with them! Use data that you have to identify what their needs are so you can create a solution that will help them.

Many wholesalers think this sounds crazy! After all, these are motivated sellers who need to get rid of their house and you are making an offer. It should be simple, right? But it's not. Motivated sellers may choose *not* to do a deal with you if they don't like you or if they don't feel that the solution is right for them. So, do some research ahead of time to help you.

Research can include:

- Pulling comps on houses in the neighborhood
- Viewing their social media
- Driving past their house (or using Google Earth to view their house)
- Listening carefully to the things they say when you are talking to them on the phone
- Making assumptions based on other sellers who have a similar demographic

When you gather all this data together, you can paint a picture of what is important to your seller: are they frustrated by the cost of the house? Are they focused on helping their family? Do they hate the neighborhood? Is their job forcing them to move? Is a recent divorce creating urgency? Are their adult children "forcing them" to sell?

Along with the research you do, you should also have a list of questions that you ask them during the negotiation that will further solidify or clarify your research.

All of this information will help you as you negotiate and close the deal. Find the key points that are important for them and show them how your solution addresses those key points. For example, someone who is focused on how much they care about their family may be willing to take a lower price for their house if they can see that selling quickly for cash will help their family sooner versus selling through a real estate agent. Or, an elderly person who isn't sure if they should do a deal with you may be more willing to do a deal if they realize that you are doing an "as-is" deal so they don't have to go through the physical effort and financial cost of updating their home.

Action Steps

1. Whenever you talk to a seller, grab a blank sheet of paper and draw two columns on it: on the left, list these data points about problems and needs of the seller that you discover in your research; on the right, list the ways that your solution addresses each problem or need. Continually revisit this list throughout your negotiation.
2. Create and memorize a list of questions that you can ask during your face-to-face meeting with them that will help you gain more information about their needs and desires.

Closers Take Action

Make sure you follow me on Facebook at @TheCloser56

CLOSING SECRET #7
PRACTICE (BUT PRACTICE
THE RIGHT THING)

Your mom was right when she said, "Practice makes perfect." At the time she may have been talking about how you played piano or how you played basketball but it applies to real estate investing too.
If you want to become better at negotiating and closing deals then practicing is the way to do it! Practicing does three things:

1. It builds the tracks in your brain that help you move along the right path.
2. It prepares you for when things go wrong in a deal to help you fix it.
3. It gives you confidence when dealing with sellers, which helps to build trust.

But, what should you practice? And how should you practice?
Ideally, you should find another wholesaler and practice with them. Set up a video camera or your phone to record your practicing and then watch the interaction. If you can't find anyone else to help you, just try practicing on your own and record yourself then play it back to review. Here are some things to practice:

- A deal conversation that goes really well. (Practice it from start to finish, including the greeting, the rapport-building, the negotiation, and the close.)
- Once you've done that several times, ask your practice partner to throw in some tricks and unexpected surprises into

the conversation. Their goal isn't to completely derail you but to get you used to dealing with surprises and get the conversation back on track.
- Practice dealing with transitions from one part of the conversation to the next.
- Practice negotiating.
- Practice closing and asking for the deal.

Always start with a few times of practicing the ideal best-case-scenario interaction because that will lay the foundation and the confidence that you need to handle situations that are less-than-ideal. And, how much should you practice? Well, people don't love practicing so most people will only do the bare minimum but the very best people practice over and over and over again until it's automatic. Practice until you're bored of it and then practice some more. Remember: even Super Bowl championship teams practice! Never stop practicing.

Action Steps

1. Make a list of things to practice.
2. Find another wholesaler and set up a regular time to get together to practice.

Closers Take Action

Make sure you follow me on Instagram at instragram.com/trob56

CLOSING SECRET #8
BE A PROFESSIONAL MIRROR

People love doing wholesale deals because it has the potential to make a lot of money, and, because it's something that can mostly be done in your comfortable clothes from home. It's like having to dress up to go to the office every day. You can be yourself without having to put on a professional façade.

However, just because you can spend most of your time in your pajamas doesn't mean you should spend all your time in your pajamas! When you meet face-to-face with sellers you'll want to be more professional.

Put yourself in your motivated seller's shoes for a moment and think about what they need: in order for them to feel good about doing the deal with you, they need the confidence that you are acting in their best interests to help them, and that you have a solution to deliver on your promise of solving their house-related problem. If you show up in ripped jeans or sweatpants, you may not give them that confidence!

It would be the same if you wanted to have your 401(k) handled by a financial advisor but that financial advisor sat down across from you in dirty, torn-up clothes. You'd wonder if they were as successful as they claimed to be.

At the same time, you don't want to show up wearing a tuxedo like James Bond if the seller is in ripped up sweatpants, either! Then you will be overdressed for the situation!

There is a middle ground: when you are meeting a seller face-to-face, be a professional. Wear nice clothes but nothing too formal. The clothes should say "I'm successful at what I do" without making the seller feel awkward.

Here are a few other tips:

- If you are dealing with motivated sellers in financial difficulty, avoid looking like a banker
- If you are dealing with elderly sellers, you may want to dress somewhat more formally (guys: consider wearing a tie) since elderly people hold a lot of respect for people wearing formal clothes
- If you are dealing with a motivated seller who is an absentee owner, wearing "business casual" clothes (dress shirts with either Dockers or nice jeans) may be a good middle ground

Ultimately you want to dress slightly better than the seller without dressing so much better than them that they feel awkward.

Of course, it's more than your clothes; I just started there because that one is an obvious "first impression" that can communicate a lot for us. It goes beyond that. There are many other ways to appear professional and seem like you have it together as a wholesaler. Here are some additional tips:

- Show up to your appointment with them on time and in a clean car.
- When you arrive at their house, look them in the eye, greet them by name, and shake their hand.
- Have all your paperwork ready and nicely organized so you're not shuffling papers.
- Thank them for meeting with you.
- Use their name throughout the meeting.
- Be respectful. Even if they have a run-down house or are hoarders, don't be disrespectful. You can point out some of a house's damage without making it seeming like it's the seller's neglect or financial situation that caused it.

Remember: Sellers have options! They can do a deal with you, they can do a deal with one of your competitors, they can sell the house themselves, they can sell through a real estate agent, or they can do nothing at all. You may be the very best option for them but if you are unprofessional, they may choose a lesser solution for themselves because they don't like or trust you.

Action Steps

1. Consider who your sellers are and select a few outfits that will give you a professional look.
2. Invest in some nice folders (just plain folders from Staples will do; it doesn't have to be fancy) that will keep your paperwork organized.
3. When you show up to a meeting, take a moment to review the person's name and make sure you use it a couple of times when you first meet them.

Closers Take Action

Make sure you check out my website at TonyTheCloser.com

Notes

_____

_____

_____

_____

_____

_____

_____

_____

_____

_____

_____

_____

_____

CLOSING SECRET #9
ATTITUDE CAN MAKE OR BREAK
THE SALE!

I hear about a lot of wholesalers who get frustrated because they can't seem to get a deal. And when I dig into what they do and how they do it, I quickly see the reason: many investors get so focused on the money they can potentially make in wholesaling and how simple wholesaling can and should be that they forget one other critical aspect of wholesaling:

Wholesaling is about helping a fellow human with a major problem they are facing with their house.

That is the attitude to have. When you're face-to-face with a seller, put aside the thought that you hope to earn your wholesaling fee and that this deal could mean a lot of money for you. Instead, adopt the mindset I introduced earlier about serving and helping someone.

It's all about attitude. When your attitude is focused on YOU and what YOU get out of the deal, you'll come across as aggressive, pushy, and greedy. You won't budge on your numbers or you'll (unconsciously) make the seller feel bad. Bad attitudes kill deals!

I love what Zig Ziglar says: "You can have everything in life you want if you will just help other people get what they want." Make that your mantra when you are face-to-face with a seller. Ask them what they want and find a way to help them get it. Yes, it might mean some give-and-take on both sides of the negotiation, but it will create more deals.

*"You can have everything in life you want,
if you will just help other people
get what they want."*

-Zig Ziglar

Something amazing will happen: sellers will open up to you and work with you when you appear to have their best interests at heart. When you care (and it shows), and when you work hard to help them, you'll end up with sellers who tearfully embrace you and thank you for helping them (even though you are making a profit on their deal) simply because you showed them that you care.

A hard-nosed wholesaler with a bad attitude might close 1 deal in 10 and feel proud that they stuck to their numbers, but a serving-focused wholesaler with a genuine attitude of helping might close 2, 3, 4, or 5 deals in 10 because they are willing to work with the seller and even accept slightly less profit because it means helping a seller while making some profit.

To do this successfully, you need to do the following:

- Know what your numbers are and understand that there is some flexibility. I'm NOT saying you should give up all profit and do this as a non-profit operation. You have every right to make money while helping people but you can do so in a way that is flexible and caring.
- Remember that you are dealing with a human being who is in a difficult situation, and consider times in your life when others have (or have not!) helped you in the way you needed.
- Be genuine and caring. Always ask yourself how you can serve others and make money doing it.

When you show someone you care about them, they'll open up to you and work with you. Now that is a way to sleep well at night, feel good about what you are doing, and put a lot of money in your pocket.

Action Steps

1. Write Zig Ziglar's quote as a reminder to yourself and repeat it every day, especially before every meeting with sellers: "You can have everything in life you want if you will just help other people get what they want."
2. Find ways that you can build flexibility into your deals (either through your numbers or through some other aspect).

Closers Take Action

Make sure you follow me on Facebook at @TheCloser56

CLOSING SECRET #10
BUILD RAPPORT

The closing of a wholesale deal starts at the opening! When you first greet a person (either on the phone or in person... but especially when in person!) build rapport with them.

Rapport is a positive feeling of engagement and familiarity. It doesn't mean that you are friends, but it means that you are friendly, polite, and are establishing a base of knowing and trusting the other person.

Rapport is all about establishing trust... which will lead to a better question/answer dialogue... which will lead to you knowing what the seller needs and the seller trusting you... which will lead to creating a solution that will help the seller... which leads to more closed deals.

Rapport is a powerful tool, but too many wholesalers skip it because they are focused on closing the deal, making their money, and moving on.

However, you should think of it like dating: you probably wouldn't ask someone to marry you the moment you met them, would you? Likely not. You'd probably go on a date, get to know them, learn about them and have them learn about you, and enjoy their company. Later you can get more serious and ultimately decide on a longer-term commitment, but the early stage of the relationship is about knowing and trusting.

And it's the same when you are doing deals with sellers.

So, how do you build rapport? Here are some simple ideas:

- Take a genuine interest in them as a human being.

- Share about yourself. You don't have to share everything but share the same kind of information you'd like to know about them.
- Make small talk. At first, this might seem like a waste of time since you just want to get to the deal, but a short discussion about simple topics like the weather can help to get into the rhythm of a rapport-building conversation.
- Ask lots of questions. Your questions don't have to be specific to the house or the deal; just ask questions about them—where they grew up, what their children's names are, what their goals in life are.
- Find topics that you can talk about that will reveal valuable details you need to know.
- Avoid topics that are controversial, such as religion and politics. Practice changing the conversation if it turns to religion or politics.

A great deal is built on a relationship. Creating rapport builds that relationship!

Action Steps

1. Learn how to make small talk. There are resources (books and videos) available to help you.
2. Learn how to ask great questions that start a conversation.
3. Always have a mental list of conversation-starting questions.
4. Remember: you are building a relationship with another human being so that you can help them! Keep that in mind always!

Closers Take Action

Make sure you follow me on Instagram at instragram.com/trob56

CLOSING SECRET #11
SHOW EMPATHY TOWARD
MOTIVATED SELLERS

Empathy is your ability to understand the feeling of the other person. It's different than sympathy, which is feeling sad for the other person. Empathy is understanding the other person.

Empathy is doing what I've prompted you to do earlier in this book: Put yourself in the other person's shoes. You're probably noticing a theme here, right? I hope so. These past few secrets are all related and they are all key components to closing more deals. You need to do all of them (and they all feed into each other so that showing empathy helps to create rapport, and creating rapport helps to show empathy.

When you have empathy, you create more trust between you and the seller but you also can create a win/win solution that helps you do more deals! So, empathy is a powerful closing secret!

To show empathy for another person do the following:

- Think about the situation they are in and try to imagine yourself in that situation.
- Listen carefully to what they say and how they say. Listen for the emotion.
- Match that emotion (but do so in a calming way). If a seller is angry, try to understand why they feel angry and feel angry too about the same situation (but don't become aggressively angry). If a seller is stressed, try to understand why they feel stressed and feel concerned about the same situation.
- Show empathy by nodding as you listen.

- Show empathy with words like "I understand" or "that sounds very difficult."
- Repeat back in your own words what you heard the other person saying.
- Ask questions like, "How did that make you feel?" or "Then what happened?"
- Show empathy by mirroring their body language.

These simple words and actions will go a long way to show empathy and build a connection.

Action Steps

1. Practice showing empathy to others. When you are listening to a family member describe a situation, be intentional about showing empathy as practice for when you are with a seller.
2. When you are hanging out with your friends, try mirroring their body language as practice for when you are with a seller.

Closers Take Action

Make sure you check out my website at TonyTheCloser.com

Notes

_____

_____

_____

_____

_____

_____

CLOSING SECRET #12
BUILD CREDIBILITY

Imagine two wholesalers: each one shows up at a motivated seller's door asking to do a deal with them; each wholesaler seems nearly identical at first; each builds rapport; each makes similar offers. In the end, which wholesaler will win the deal? Answer: the one who seems most credible.

Credibility is when you have built up a reputation that proves you can be trusted. When two wholesalers are side by side and seem nearly identical, the one with the most credibility will win the deal, always. That's because credibility will make the wholesaler seem like a more trustworthy expert.

Think of the most credible people you've dealt with, perhaps including a doctor or a college professor, and other professions like that. What makes them credible? Their credibility is related to:

- Their education (think of how a professor or a doctor has many years of schooling)
- The clothes they wear (think of commercials for medicine that show an actor in a white doctor's lab coat)
- The books they've produced (a professor must regularly publish, in journals and textbooks and even write their own books)
- How often they are mentioned or quoted by others
- Being a "thought leader" in their field
- Testimonials and case studies by other people
- Proof of past successes

In this chapter we've been comparing two imaginary wholesalers but here's something you already know: there's probably more than two wholesalers in your area, right? It's not just you and one other wholesaler... there are probably many. Get added credibility to help you build trust with motivated sellers, and that will help you do more deals.

Action Steps

1. Think of the most credible people in your life and what they do to earn that credibility. See how you can do the same.
2. Constantly collect testimonials, case studies, and other proof to establish your credibility.

Closers Take Action

Make sure you follow me on Facebook at @TheCloser56

Notes

_____
_____
_____
_____
_____
_____
_____
_____
_____
_____

CLOSING SECRET #13
QUESTIONS

If I could arm you with just one tool as a wholesaler and tell you to use this particular tool more than you are to do more deals, this would be it: ask questions. Questions are one of the most powerful tools you have in your arsenal as a wholesaler.

Questions serve three key purposes:

1. Questions show that you are interested in the other person
2. Questions help the seller like you even more
3. Questions give you the answers you need to be a better negotiator

One of the best-kept secrets of the most popular and beloved people is: they ask better questions. People who are the most beloved and the most charismatic are the ones who seem like they are genuinely interested in the other person. When we ask better questions, we show that we are interested in the other person, and that makes the seller like us even more.

And, as the person answers your questions, they reveal pieces of information that help you negotiate more effectively. Good questions get to the root of the problem and discover need without the seller feeling pressured. Ask open-ended questions that draw out problems, concerns, and needs that the seller is feeling.

Good questions are open-ended so they invite a detailed response (instead of just a yes or no response). For example: "What are two problems you're experiencing with your home that I could help solve?" Or, "If you could wave a magic wand and get the perfect solution, what would it look like?"

Learn to ask more questions; learn to ask better questions. Do both of those things over and over and you'll do more deals.

Action Steps

1. Create and memorize a list of questions that extracts the answers you need to know.
2. Practice asking these questions.
3. Always be on the lookout for great questions and collect them like a kid collects baseball cards!

Closers Take Action

Make sure you follow me on Instagram at instragram.com/trob56

Notes

_____
_____
_____
_____
_____
_____
_____
_____
_____
_____
_____
_____
_____

CLOSING SECRET #14
BECOME A PROBLEM SOLVER

A wholesaler walked out of a failed negotiation shaking his head. He thought he had the deal locked up but then the seller wouldn't close in the end.

If only I had a nickel for every time a wholesaler complained about that exact thing happening! Many wholesalers go into negotiations wondering what it will take to get the seller to do a deal with them, and they leave the failed negotiation frustrated that they couldn't get the deal done.

I'll tell you the answer: stop wondering what it will take to get the seller to do a deal with you and instead start asking yourself: "What problem does the seller have that I can solve?"

Find out what issue you can solve. Find out needs they have so you can offer solutions. Find problems and solve them. That's it. It's not hidden from you; it's plain and simple: the seller has a problem. If you can figure out what that problem is and solve it, you'll do the deal. If ever you fail at a negotiation, it's either because you didn't figure out what the problem was, or you didn't create a compelling enough solution for the problem.

Bonus tip: You can go into negotiations with an upper hand because you probably have a general idea of what their problem likely is! A motivated seller in financial distress probably can't afford to continue living in their house; a motivated seller who is an absentee owner probably feels stress about the cost and effort required to keep the house; etc. Of course, the specific problem and a specific solution will need to be identified but you can arm yourself with likelihoods before going into the deal and that will give you a head start when you are seeking out a solution.

Action Steps

1. Think of the most common problems that your sellers might have and create solutions for those problems. (Of course you can make adjustments during the negotiation but these solutions are good starting points.)
2. Think back on the deals you've negotiated but didn't close: can you think of what the problems were that the seller had that you didn't address?

Closers Take Action

Make sure you check out my website at TonyTheCloser.com

CLOSING SECRET #15
LISTEN

It's ironic that people think they come across as more caring and authoritative when they talk. The opposite is true! You come across as more caring and more authoritative when you listen.

People love to talk, so when you listen to someone, you allow them to communicate to you *and feed you information that you can use to close the deal!*

As they say: we have two ears and one mouth, so we should listen twice as much as we speak. That's a good rule of thumb.

Pay attention to conversations you have (whether just personal conversations or when you are talking to a seller) and note who does more of the speaking and what the result of the conversation is! You will be surprised that the person who listens often has more power and control over the conversation and comes across as more credible and helpful.

It's a simple tip; I don't have much more to say about it! Just LISTEN!!!

Action Steps

1. Pay attention in your conversations to note who does more talking.
2. Remind yourself to do less talking when with a seller.
3. Listen actively to get more clues to help you close the deal.

Closers Take Action

Make sure you follow me on Facebook at @TheCloser56

CLOSING SECRET #16
VALIDATE

I've been recommending that you ask a lot of questions and listen to the answers. You've also read that you should do your research and look for problems that you can solve. All of this is really powerful… if you are asking the right questions, hearing the right answers, and solving the right problems.

The problem is, wholesalers don't always do that. They ask a question but get an answer and move on; they hear an answer and misinterpret it; they think they hear the problem and solve it only to find out it's the wrong problem.

All of the research, preparation, questions, and problem-seeking that you do will only work if you validate what you are learning. You have to make sure that you are hearing the person correctly and getting accurate information that you understand.

Each one of us approaches every interaction with our own preconceived notions, and we view the world through our own lens. When we research and build rapport and have empathy, we are attempting to see the world through someone else's eyes but we need to make sure what we are seeing is accurate.

Often, sellers will say one thing but mean something else. They aren't trying to lie to us but they may have conscious or unconscious reasons for giving one reason for selling their house and not giving another reason. For example, they might say something because that's what they think you want to hear; or, they may not tell you something else because they are embarrassed about the other situation. Or it could simply be a situation that they don't speak English very well or they can't articulate themselves very well.

That's where validation comes in. Validation ensures that we understand correctly. You need to always dig deep and validate to make sure you are getting the full story. To validate, do the following:

- Listen carefully.
- Watch the person's body language: does their body language match up with what they are saying?"
- Listen in between the lines.
- Ask questions that dig deeper, such as: "Tell me more about that."
- Repeat back what you just heard to the person who said it: "So what I'm hearing is… [then restate in your own words]… Would you say that's accurate?"
- Write down what they said. (This shows that you are paying attention; it also helps you to keep all the information straight, especially if you leave the house and need to review your notes later.)

Action Steps

1. Memorize a list of questions that will help you to dig deep.
2. When you talk to people throughout your day (whether sellers or other investors or even your barber or hairdresser) practice validating what you are hearing and repeating back what they just told you.

Closers Take Action

Make sure you follow me on Instagram at instragram.com/trob56

CLOSING SECRET #17
SHOW VALUE

If you do all of the things I've described so far in this book—from adopting a mindset of service and preparing; to asking great questions and seeking out problems—then it will set you up for this next step… show value.

At some point during the negotiation you will start to tip the scales from gathering information to presenting a solution. That solution should be the perfect answer to the most burning problem that the seller is facing, and all of the secrets described in this book so far will help you create the perfect solution.

To create a perfect solution you need to show that the solution you are offering has amazing value to the seller.

Value is when someone exchanges something they have for something else that is worth just as much or more. It's like the concept of a return on investment (except, in this case, the seller isn't investing money; they're investing their time and effort to solve a problem).

Your solution needs to provide value by showing that you will help them come out ahead at the end of the transaction.

Many wholesalers get caught up with a focus on dollars and sense: they think of value in terms of money only, so they can't see who their solution of a below-market offer on a house will be valuable to the seller… but it can be! When you listen to the seller and hear what their emotional hot buttons are, you'll discover that money may not be as important as other things:

Saving time and effort
- Getting out from the crushing burden of the house
- Putting the memories of the house behind them
- Avoiding a foreclosure
- Putting an end to the stresses of being a landlord
- Getting cash to solve a problem right away (instead of waiting for the house to be sold on the market)

These are just a few of the many ways that your solution can provide value to sellers. Now, listen to your sellers and ask questions to find out what their true problem is, then present a solution that helps your sellers feel like they are coming out ahead.

When you do that, you create an irresistible offer that sellers will agree to!

Action Steps

1. List the different types of value do your sellers need? (Time? Effort? Saving their reputation? Saving their credit?)
2. Figure out how to present a solution that highlights the value your sellers need.

Closers Take Action

Make sure you check out my website at TonyTheCloser.com

CLOSING SECRET #18
CLARITY

You've worked hard to get to know a seller and understand their reasons for selling. Now you present your offer. There's one thing that a lot of wholesalers do at this point, and that is: confuse the message. They make their offer but present it in such a confusing way that the seller says no and the wholesaler leaves the negotiation in defeat.

When you make your offer to a seller and ask them to do the deal with you, you need to be clear. Clarity will help you get more deals and confusion will only drive sellers away.

That's because a confused mind says "no." Sellers may know, like, and trust you but they only know, like, and trust you to a certain point; their brain is always on the lookout for opportunities to get out of the deal or for reasons not to trust someone... and a confusing presentation will make them think: "I don't understand this deal and therefore I could be ripped off." So they will say no.

Figure out the clearest way to make your offer. Use words the seller understands. Don't rush through your offer. Don't assume the seller knows exactly what you are talking about. Don't use fancy words to make yourself seem knowledgeable.

Just talk slowly, plainly, simply, and honestly. Write it down in a way that the seller can see and understand. Pause periodically to make sure the seller understands what you are saying.

Action Steps

1. Write out your closing presentation (or record yourself and have it transcribed). Then look for ways to cut it down and clarify it.
2. Practice presenting your offer in a clear way. Practice over and over, recording yourself and reviewing it.

Closers Take Action

Make sure you follow me on Facebook at @TheCloser56

CLOSING SECRET #19
CREATE SCARCITY

You've talked to the seller and you've heard their problems and you've created the perfect solution for them. Problem is, human nature kicks in at this point. Human nature is all about stasis; it's all about familiarity. Human nature doesn't want us to make a decision (even when that decision is logically in our best interest!) Human nature wants to avoid commitment! (Yes it's crazy but we're all like that!)

The wholesaler needs to help the seller overcome this problem in themselves, and the way to do that is by introducing scarcity: scarcity means that the solution is not going to be available for long, and therefore the person must act fast in order to get it, or they will lose out on the opportunity to benefit.

If the seller thinks that your offer will be around forever, their human nature kicks in and they believe that they will be okay to delay a decision until later. They may call you up in a week or a month or a year and decide to do the deal, or they may never call you at all.

However, if the seller thinks that your offer will go away, their human nature kicks in and they realize they'd better get it while they can or else they will lose out. Therefore, a sense of scarcity creates urgency to act. Without scarcity, many sellers won't do the deal.

How do you create scarcity? Here are two simple ways:

1. Make an offer only valid for a certain period of time. You can decide how long your offer is valid for—perhaps as long as you are in front of the seller, or just for 24 hours. The shorter the time period, the better.

2. Tell the seller that you only do so many deals each week and you are almost at your limit. If they don't act now, they may not be able to do the deal with you and they'll have to wait.

After that time period, you simply tear up the offer and move on. If sellers know that you are willing to do that, they will be more likely to move forward. (It may sound harsh but you are actually helping the seller by doing this!)

Action Steps

1. Identify all the ways that you can create scarcity in your deal.
2. Remind yourself during the negotiation to introduce the concept of scarcity and warn the seller that the deal won't be around forever.

Closers Take Action

Make sure you follow me on Instagram at instragram.com/trob56

Notes

_____

_____

_____

_____

_____

_____

_____

_____

CLOSING SECRET #20
TIMING IS EVERYTHING

There are many places where wholesalers can mess up during the negotiation (and that's why I wrote this book: to help you know the secrets and strategies to master closing a wholesale deal!)… but one of the most common ways that a wholesaler can mess up during the negotiation is by getting the timing wrong.

Timing is everything! If you make an offer too soon, the seller will probably say no and show you the door. The problem is, wholesalers want to do the deal and move on.

Want to know the better way? Think back to when you were a kid at Christmas. If you were like most children, you saw the tree go up at your house and then you started thinking about what? Presents! As the days passed and Christmas drew near, your level of excitement and anticipation rose. You could not get to Christmas Day fast enough! You practically begged to open gifts early, right? Imagine what would happen if your parents relented and you actually got to open your gifts early? Well, even though the wait is painful, you'd actually ruin the fun of Christmas, wouldn't you?

It's the same with sellers: as a wholesaler you want to get to the deal soon but sellers need to be prepped, and the relationship needs to be built up and the anticipation needs to be heightened… only when the seller is ready to say yes (as giddy and excited for Christmas as a child would be!), that's when you present the offer. Do it too early and the seller may push back and say "no."

Instead, keep going back to the other secrets in this book—asking questions, listening, validating—and you will build the anticipation. Watch for signs from the seller that they are ready to hear an offer (signs include body language that leans in, as well as questions about how to get started). Then, only make your offer when the seller is ready to say yes! Timing is everything and moving in too soon will harm the deal.

Action Steps

1. Make a reminder to yourself to wait before you present the deal. If you create a deal checklist that you follow during the negotiation, include a checkbox that reminds you to wait.
2. On your next deal, try waiting for a while longer before making your offer. See what happens.

Closers Take Action

Make sure you check out my website at TonyTheCloser.com

Notes

_____

_____

_____

_____

_____

_____

_____

_____

_____

_____

_____

_____

_____

CLOSING SECRET #21
FOLLOW UP

I've got good news and bad news... and MORE bad news for you!

The bad news is that some sellers won't make an appointment when you ask them for one.

The other bad news is that even if you do get a face-to-face meeting with them, some sellers won't do a deal.

But here's the good news: Just because they said no to the first meeting on the first call, or just because they said no to doing a deal when you were face-to-face with them, doesn't mean you should delete them and move on.

On the contrary! Some people's default position is just to say "no" no matter what, even if it's in their best interest to say yes.

The secret? Follow-up. Constantly. Relentlessly. And always with a mindset of helping them (after all, you have a great service that can help them!)

As many as half of all wholesalers will never make another call to a seller after they've said "no" to an appointment. That's great because it means that there are many sellers out there who have turned away other wholesalers but who you could do a deal with if you only try them a second... third... or fourth time!

You need to follow up with sellers because maybe on the day that you first spoke with them, they were distracted by something else or they didn't feel the acute pain of their problem that day... but following up again and again will catch them on a day when they are focused on how challenging their house problem is and how you can help them.

Action Steps

1. Create a follow-up system that reminds you to call people back again and again.
2. Be relentless. Call people back regularly; if they won't do a deal with you this week, try next week… then next month… then the month after.

Closers Take Action

Make sure you follow me on Facebook at @TheCloser56

NEXT STEP

What's the next step for you? It's simple. If you want to know how to close more wholesale deals and finally elevate to the level you know is possible for you, then go to **TonyTheCloser.com** right now to learn how you can become a master wholesale closer even with zero experience!

ABOUT THE AUTHOR

Tony Robinson is a father, son, mentor, sales trainer and now author! Growing up in the city of Brotherly Love, Philadelphia, Tony was no stranger to the crime-ridden streets of the inner city. Later in childhood, Tony moved to a small town in North Carolina where he was exposed to more crime and domestic violence. This was the beginning of Tony's fight with life: he knew he had to do whatever it took to create a different narrative. With a strong work ethic instilled by his parents, Tony used his experiences as motivation and envisioned a life where his dreams come true.

Seeing sports as his escape, he focused all his attention on playing football and becoming the very best. Throughout his high school and collegiate football careers, Tony became an All-American, breaking numerous records—some of which he still holds today. His hard work, persistence, determination and innate capacity for success turned his childhood dream into reality and he became a Linebacker for the Seattle Seahawks NFL Football team. Unfortunately, his dream was shattered when a pre-season injury permanently sidelined him before his first season with the team. Tony didn't let this stop him, though, so he turned a chance meeting with NASCAR team owner Rick Hendricks into a fulfilling sales career within the Hendrick Automotive Group organization.

Turns out, Tony's skills honed on the football field combined with his Business Administration degree from Carson Newman College, gave him the tools he needed to shine as a car salesman. In his first month, he sold more than 23 vehicles, and continued to break sales records year after year, even achieving the top honors of becoming a member of two exclusive clubs for top salespeople—the President's and Chairman's Clubs.

After a few years of success, several roadblocks presented themselves. Yet, in spite of an unsuccessful business, a failed marriage, and loss of freedom, Tony's determination and undefeated mindset allowed him to turn any obstacle into an opportunity for improvement. Tony took responsibility for his decisions, repaired broken relationships and leveled up his thinking and positioned himself for greater success while helping others.

Over the years, Tony has closed more than 1000 deals and generated more than 10 million dollars in auto and real estate sales. Today, Tony, along with his partner, Max Maxwell, run a multi-million dollar real estate investing company where Tony uses his closing skills to do more deals than most people even dream of! It's no secret that his commitment and his belief that "it's not how many times you fall but how you 'get yo ass up'," has led him to educate others and share his 21 Proven Secrets to Close that changed his life and can change yours too!

Made in the USA
Las Vegas, NV
16 August 2023

76182539R00035